For the parents that raised me to redefine strong- Keith and Julie

Dedicated to the SEE US Movement. Founded by Courtney Place in February 2018, the mission is to spread awareness about female athletes being underrepresented, sexualized, and judged on appearance rather than ability.

Facebook, Instagram & Twitter:
@seeusmovement

Courtney fell in love with volleyball and basketball. She carried around a volleyball wherever she went and shot hoops for hours.

Denae enjoyed playing football. She could catch really well and throw extremely far. Playing football made Denae feel happy.

Hanna fell in love with the game of volleyball. The sport made her realize that she was very competitive.

Lexi dreamed of playing volleyball in college. As a young girl, she was a little uncoordinated, but was determined to work hard and make her dreams come true.

Rachel grew up watching her older siblings play sports. She knew from a young age that she wanted to be an athlete. Rachel quickly found her love for softball and volleyball.

As Courtney grew up, people started to notice her biggest insecurity—her large feet. She was not able to wear cute shoes like the other girls. Courtney felt left out.

Denae was becoming better and better at football. Eventually the boys in her class complained to their teacher. They started calling Denae a gorilla because of her athletic abilities and the hair on her arms and legs.

Hanna started playing volleyball on a traveling club team. She gained big muscles in her legs. Hanna became insecure about how her body was changing.

Lexi grew taller than everyone in her class. She was teased about her height. This made Lexi feel sad about her size.

Rachel had always felt shy, afraid of change, and unsure of herself. It was hard for her to see her full potential. Rachel was afraid of making mistakes.

During a basketball game, Courtney made a three-point shot. The opponents' crowd started to yell, "BIG FEEEET!"

After giving up football, Denae became an incredible volleyball player. A couple of boys came up to her after a match and told her, "We only come to your games to watch your butt." Denae became very self-conscious.

After time spent with her faith and family, Hanna was able to accept her body and became the person she wanted to be.

In eighth grade, Lexi started playing varsity volleyball. Older team members were not kind. Lexi started thinking about purposely playing poorly to give the older girls more playing time.

Rachel realized that her love for playing sports was more about being part of a team. She decided to play softball and volleyball in college.

During one of the biggest games of the year, Courtney's teammate set her perfectly resulting in a kill. As her team celebrated, the opposing fans chanted, "SHE'S A MAN."

After Denae and her high school volleyball team competed at two state tournaments, the lack of media coverage compared to their less-than-average football team made the girls sad.

Once Hanna arrived at college, she quickly experienced the spotlight of being a college athlete. She battled with what she should look like in a volleyball uniform, bringing back old insecurities.

Lexi was told multiple times that she was only good at sports because she was black. Her hard work, passion, and commitment were ignored.

As Rachel's athletic career came to an end, she struggled with negative body image. She found herself comparing characteristics of others with her own on social media.

Courtney was recognized for achieving 2000 points in her career. Although a big accomplishment, she was told that her points did not have as much meaning because she was playing against women; and women's basketball is like "watching paint dry."

Hanna found the importance of focusing on the things she loved to do. She chose to stop stressing about her appearance. Hanna's love for volleyball helped her become the best version of herself.

Lexi went to college, worked hard, and played the sport she loved. She faced adversity, but Lexi's determination led to success.

Rachel realized that her negative views of herself were only societal expectations. She looked back on the strong foundation built by being a teammate, friend, sister, daughter, and aunt. Rachel realized that she was **enough**.

Courtney found that many female athletes have stories similar to her own. She founded the SEE US Movement to empower girls and women to be confident and strong.

Denae realized that she was not alone in having self-doubts. Through volleyball she found the confidence to be herself. As her college career ended, SEE US gave Denae the opportunity to inspire others.

These five women's stories are very different but share similarities. Although their struggles varied, their responses remained the same. After each obstacle knocked them down, they got right back up. Courtney learned that the way other people talked about her did not define her. Denae learned to find self-worth. Hanna learned to love herself. Lexi learned not to give up, no matter the circumstances. Rachel learned that she was more than her appearance.

You might see yourself in these characters. You might be going through something similar. If so, continue to rise up; continue to redefine strong.

"Strong to me means fighting for personal passions when it feels like you are fighting alone. It is easy to stand up when people are cheering and constantly being supportive. At some point, however, each person needs the inner strength to individually rise up. Once this self-confidence is gained, the possibilities are endless."

-Courtney Place, founder of the
SEE US Movement

"Strong to me is not only being able to mentally, emotionally, and physically persevere, but to also empower and enable others to do it as well."

-Ashley Denae

 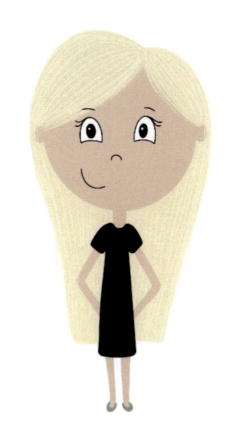

"Strong means to fight for what you truly believe in, and sometimes it means continuing through a hard battle when nobody is in your corner cheering for you; however, for me, I found my biggest cheerleader to be Christ. Matthew 26:41 said it best, '...The spirit is willing, but the body is weak.' I am a firm believer that you can do **anything** you set your mind to. The only person limiting you, is you."

-Hanna Justesen

"Strong is living fearless. It's not letting the little things that don't matter bother you. It's being **YOU** in every moment of life and never changing yourself due to tough circumstances. It's continuing to fight for what you are passionate about even when doubt creeps in. Strong is never giving up and always standing up for what you believe in."

-Lexi Scott

"To me, strong is standing firm in who you are and the positive ripple you are capable of creating. Real strength comes from within. You can show your strength by treating others with kindness, offering a listening ear, lending a hand, and empowering self-worth. Most importantly, real strength is shown in the way you care for and uplift yourself. Your strength is unique to you—everyone has a different strength to offer."

-Rachel Mathias

Made in the USA
Middletown, DE
04 September 2020

17793455R00020